AFTER THE RACE: Friendly Street Poets 34

Janine Baker writes poetry with environmental and social themes, influenced by an itinerant upbringing in many places around Australia and in Papua New Guinea. She works as a marine scientist, and writes poetry in brief spurts. Janine has had more than 115 poems published intermittently during the past decade, in journals, books and e-zines in Australia, and more recently in USA. A first collection, *Circus Earth*, was published in 2008 by Friendly St Poets Inc. and Wakefield Press (South Australia).

A.M. Sladdin, an Adelaidean, runs a gallery-bookshop in the Mid North town of Saddleworth. She won Adelaide University's 2005 Bundey Prize for English Verse with one of her MA (Creative Writing) poems. She has been published in several anthologies (her one favourable review by J.M. Coetzee!) and is currently undertaking her PhD. Since learning to write she has done so.

AFTER THE RACE
Friendly Street Poets 34

Edited by

Janine Baker and A.M. Sladdin

§

Friendly Street Poets

Friendly Street Poets Incorporated
PO Box 3697
Norwood
South Australia 5000
friendlystreetpoets.org.au

Wakefield Press
1 The Parade West
Kent Town
South Australia 5067
www.wakefieldpress.com.au

First published 2010

Cover photograph by L.G. Sladdin
Cover design by Marc Jusserand, Creative Hand
Edited by Janine Baker and A.M. Sladdin, Friendly Street Poets Inc.
Typeset by Clinton Ellicott, Wakefield Press
Printed in Australia by Griffin Digital, Adelaide

ISBN 978 1 86254 883 1

Government
of South Australia

Arts SA

Friendly Street Poets Inc. is supported
by the **South Australian Government**
through **Arts SA**.

fox creek
wines

CONTENTS

THANK YOU

Thank you to the poets who read at city and regional meetings
and submitted their work; thanks to the supportive audiences;
and thanks also to the poets who submitted entries to our competitions
throughout the year.

Thank you for the continuing support of Arts SA who keep our
publishing program financially viable.

ACKNOWLEDGEMENT

Friendly Street Poets acknowledges the Kaurna people
as the original owners and custodians of the Adelaide Plains

PREFACE

Inaugurated in 1975, Friendly Street Poets is the longest running open reading poetry group in the southern hemisphere. Ongoing passion for poetic expression binds together this large group of people. The collective spirit and egalitarian ethos of our community has ensured that the nurturing, support and promotion of South Australian poetry persists and continues to develop and flourish, in the face of life's many challenges in the 21st century.

Poems for this year's Reader came from 11 city meetings, regional readings at Salisbury, Murray Bridge, Noarlunga, and two meetings at Port Adelaide. Also, throughout the year, a number of competitions were run by Friendly Street, with publication of the winning entries as part of the prizes.

Friendly Street has always aimed to foster new and emerging voices, as well as provide a respected and reliable platform for established poets. Representing regional poets, who cannot attend the city meetings on the first Tuesday of each month, is a newer and equally important aim of Friendly Street. With those goals in mind, more than 20% of the content of this year's Reader comes from new poets and regional poets.

Selection for the Reader is never an easy task, and many fine poems almost made the cut, alongside those which stood out as works deserving a permanent place in print. From the broad melting pot of entries, we distilled what we hope is a classic mix of country and city, love and despair, family and friends, frustration and delight, respect for the earth, and ever prevailing insight into the human condition.

Janine Baker and Alice Sladdin

MIDNIGHT

midnight
mid-January
I discard
those promises
along with your empties

DAVID TERELINCK
Winner – Tanka: Japanese Poetry Competition 2009

DAYS

Tree shadows and winter greens of farms are earthy
oppositions in the sun. A herd of dairy
grazing, a bull in seclusion. And now
I'm looking at the sun descending, icy
on the dam, and somewhere in between
a day took place. There's a book the size of poems
and a silver plate with vines, salvaged for a coin.
There's a foal galloping, gangly, kicking
up the grass, the air itself like glass.
There's a stranger where we struck up like light
as if there were secrets in the atoms,
in the air. There's town and country and white
blossoming trees and cold creeks running over
their banks, deep in the vein of winter.

KAREN BLAYLOCK
Read at Salisbury Writers Festival, August 2009

1905

This photograph of a small town
has shown up here in front of me
through the snowflakes of 1905.
The only person to be seen is
somewhere in the middle distance:
a woman in a long dress who
could be walking along the road
but, as she moves towards me
has to be riding a bicycle.
She moves past me. Out of sight.
There might have been specks of
people in what the white whited
into the far white distance but
they're no longer there. Here.
There are no people in this town.
Chimneys are their headstones.

GRAHAM ROWLANDS

MUSINGS OF SUMMER

For one more summer and one less
the breeze is gauzy wings
no longer arid nor as yet damp
fluttering in my hair
and those days that have unrolled
like a treasure map are curling in now;
one more summer and one less
to go bare foot
sluice away heat in a spearmint sea.
But the sun is northward
and for one more summer and one less
I anticipate those first drops
that springboard from the ti tree,
ball dust into poppy seeds of clay
darken the earth with rain scent.
For one more year and one less
I want to press my ear against the tank
hear water trickle into water
feel autumn's bristles on my face
as they sweep in winter
for one more year with no hint of my last.

DAVID COOKSON
Read at Port Noarlunga, September 2009

GIFT OF AUTUMN

Not a hidden partridge to be seen.
No fruits, no seeds,
just a thousand, thousand
heart shaped Manchurian leaves,
fibrillating in the icy breeze
and the cold face
of the dawn time moon.

Eclipsed by the rising sun,
a street of ruby lanterns,
is briefly lit, to float and spin
in gravity's gyroscope,
as the sap snaps.

One rescued in a stoop
for a lover's palm,
not the actual thing, snatched
like Shelley's from a funeral pyre
to carry in a silken sling,
but a simulacral token
pointing like an arrow of desire
straight to the heart.

PAUL WILKINS

WINTER'S GRAND ENTRANCE

Blanketing the soil
deciduous trees retire,
starved from summer's heat.

Weathered leaves spiral
fluidly towards the ground,
preparing new soil.

A soft moist air blows,
its whispering to nature;
winter's lullaby.

ANDREW ELLERY

BARE

This day is the first I walk our way.
There is no sheltering sky.
No birds on the wire.
Streets are empty.
Cars are left with space aplenty.
Traffic poles are black holes.
Store shelves are barren.
Tables, unmarked fountains
chairs, scattered seed
plates, masks set free
cutlery, fingers of useless utility
glass, sand castles scorned
menu bleached wordless form;
But here my bacon arrives freshly fried
bringing home the day we died.

MICHÈLE SAINT-YVES

RELEASE

Rain: tin roof. Sounds like
skin grafted on gurgling wounds,
rasping with relief.

MICHÈLE SAINT-YVES

AUTUMN RAINFALL

the hum-drum of rain against tin
a croaky-voiced wind scrabbling through the trees

finally
      the heavens are being plucked
the stars flung out across the rooftops & garden beds
      soaking into the sediment between paving stones

a season of regret
      spent in the blast & shrift of heat
      that made the front lawn fast & leaves age
      as the coils of water restrictions entangled & choked

but finally
      it makes landfall   the rescue ship   the wet breeze
      articulating the loaded tone & variation
      the welcome repetition of watery song
struck against stone
      & echoing in the tubular bells of guttering pipes
         rinsing out the ash & burnt remains
         of a summer haze

JULIET A. PAINE

CERTAINTY

If I had told you
about the spider-web
which bridged the space
between two small branches
on the Prunus pissardi
I'd come upon
that cold morning
on the path across the garden
and if I'd spoken of its spare mystery,
the threads strung from its bridge line,
each silk strand spun with dewdrops,
each glistening sharp and fine,
that web would have drawn you in
and you would have marvelled
at its mathematical precision,
the clarity of design,
and would have pictured it
like an unspoken whisper
and carried it with you
as I have done.

ELAINE BARKER

TRAPPED

Back and forth
the bug spins
within the perimeter of the page
a new paddock
the whiteness shows the limits
outlines a fence
a sense of something different on the other side
good or bad, does it matter?
Left, right, left again
pausing to rub its legs
to think.
Right, left, right again
still trapped within imaginary bounds.
Down, up, down again
scurrying in lines
pause
rub.
Up, down, up again
pause
think
then remembered
wings.

LILLIANA ROSE

WET SEASON NIGHT

Cicadas sing in the sultry night
and the air is thick with invisible moisture.

Insects swarm around lights and windows
knocking on the wire with fluttering wings.

A house on stilts stands like a metal alien
protecting a car behind long limbs.

Next to the stairs paw-paw trees grow
their pendulous fruits like pregnant breasts.

Inside a room people sip their drinks
while an overhead fan beats an even rhythm.

Tension builds in an electric atmosphere
and all await the approaching storm.

Flashes of pink lightning bring a return to day
and for a brief moment the night is gone.

Explosive thunder rattles the louvers
shaking the house in a display of power.

Heavy rain pounds on the iron roof
and all talking stops as the heavens speak.

Suddenly, the storm has passed
and water cascades over flooded gutters.

As the world of insects begins a new chorus
the ringing downpipes clear their throats.

Bright green frogs with yellow mouths
celebrate with croaks the change of season.

DAVID BAILES

ICON

A crouching river red-gum:
its muscular, naked torso
marble-white. One leg
anchored, locked buttock-
deep in the riverbank. With
its other leg – a contorting
branch that doubles-back,
tucked hard against its body –
it levers, flexing, straining,
struggling to rend itself free.
And all the while its netted,
frantic arms rail against
a mesh of swarming green.

THOM SULLIVAN

THE DAY IN SUMMER

The Morning
Bright yellow splashes wall.
Birds chirp, stretch and ruffle.
Nature reaches for God's call.
Subtle sounds merge to muffle.

The Afternoon
Piquant compressed second-hand air.
Highways of ant-line cavalcade.
Bright light and western sky aflare.
Slight breeze whispers swell of shade.

The Gathering
People eat, view, talk, listen and read.
Undoing the knot of daily bustle.
Resting light times burning need.
Undoing routines echo of muscle.

NEIL STEPHENS

purple drifting down –
jacaranda bells
herald Advent, waiting time

DAWN COLSEY

STAR CYCLE

You slip, unheld
from sky to deep ocean,
or so it seems.
Juicy orb, fluorescent to amber,
crafter of spirits, minister to life.

Tempted, like Icarus
in wide-eyed fervor,
I know not to touch,
only to worship from cold
dampened shores.

I grieve the world's turning,
today's unique greatness
and the beauty of believing
forever exists in your wake.

CHRISTINA BELL
Read at Murray Bridge, September 2009

LEARNING TO READ

I'm not as dyslexic as I was;
my reading of the country's getting better.
Along the bush track, I keep an eye open
for birds I've come to know –
mulga parrots, spinifex pigeons,
spiny-cheeked honeyeaters.
I recognise trees and grasses
and what they're good for –
the swamp grass, whose seeds
were staple diet in the olden days,
corkwood, whose bark has medicinal uses,
mulga for woomeras and boomerangs,
beanwood for shields and carrying dishes,
ironwood, the best firewood –
once alight it doesn't go out
but keeps burning slowly
with good heat and little smoke.

In the outstation camp, when I arrive,
people are walking around slowly,
searching the ground. Apme.
A snake track's been seen.
The snake might still be around.
He beckons me, Aboriginal way,
with palm-down scooping motion,
and points at the ground worn bare
by the coming and going of vehicles.
Apmeke impatje, snake track.
I look intently but see nothing;
to me the ground is a clean slate.
He bends down to point more closely.
Is he playing a trick on me,
pointing at something that's not there?

Then we squat, and with his finger
almost touching it, I finally make out
the small crescent-shaped indentation
in the thin layer of loose sand
on top of the compacted earth.

And I understand, now,
that the snake doesn't drag itself
along, leaving a wavy track,
but coils and grips, coils and grips,
leaving spaced marks at right angles
to its direction of travel.
And I learn, too, from this track –
which was invisible to my eye
but like words on a page to the others –
that I'm still a foreigner here,
a schoolchild learning basic literacy,
not yet fluent in the land's language,
still learning to decipher its writing.

JOHN PFITZNER

JENNIFER JANDRUWANDA

Artist   Musician   Poet

Stolen from the cradle
of spiritual land and
your mother tongue shunned
as white man's words ruled the land

slender fingers extended
like an eagle's wing in flight
danced on the ivory keyboard and
the pianist composed poetic lyrics
as Mother Nature whispered
birdsong lullabies accompanied
by the orchestral of rustling gum leaves
and ghost eucalyptus peels bark skin
reclaimed by the earth's womb.

COLLEEN SWEENEY

WAKEHURST PARKWAY

The world is cold and black, sad. My light's on but makes no difference. The journey is long and pointless, blunt in a social wasteland of in-laws and accretions. Vulnerable astride the bike. Cars. Obstacles. Police. Speed. Senses are stretched as the long black strip lined with white is endured until the goal. Focus on the goal. Finish quickly. Do what we must. Duty driven. Driven duty. Duty on two wheels. Have duty will travel.

Scintillating colours grab focus. Birds cross, on a different path. Bright sharp sounds lead in the foreground as branches wave. Cicadas and crickets constitute the choir. Sun and shadow, light and shade. Shades of greens and browns, blacks and greys, reds and purples and more. Textures of trees, scrub and grass. Pockets of warmth, then coolness too. Smells of flowers, eucalypti and swamp, growth and decay. Power hums beneath my bum and the wind pushes and plays. A gloved fist punches the sky while Yahoo! adds to nature's song. I am present now, alive.

HAKIM OERTON
Read at Murray Bridge, September 2009

FIRE FLIES

Through Louisiana's lowland forest
the Wild Azalea Trail laid out my way
by mossy bogs and wooded slopes adorned
with moistland vegetation all profuse.

I gloried in this wayside new to me,
its visual textures and its odours fresh,
a counterpoint to paths I'd trod before,
a revel for a soul upon the loose.

For me, from names and preconceptions free,
the blossoms, leaves and forms entranced my eye
with beauties freshly new, to me unknown,
and mysteries flowing from an undelved grace.

With one last stretch of forestland to walk,
as I was coming to the edge of town.
The day out-strode my steps as darkness fell
and once again I cursed my time-slowed pace.

With artificial light I groped my way
through shadows dark and bushland ever dense
when down the trail another walker came,
as then it seemed, bearing another light –

– but then another! Then came many more
and closer now to hand! Fire flies they were
but brighter far than any seen or dreamt
by me, which filled me with a new delight.

I made my way along entranced by light
and feeling now that things had come out right:
with faster steps I'd not have seen this sight
that brightened up my heart as well as night.

LAWRENCE JOHNSON
Read at Port Noarlunga, September 2009

HAZE

Under this hazy air
the sea lies quiet,
it makes no wavelet on the sand,
no sigh.
In the morning light it is still pale
yet lilac luminous as a polished stone;
an agate sea making light its own,
lying in the arm of velvet,
smoke veiled hills, secretly
touching the sky far-off
beyond our view.

A thousand, thousand weepings
in this sea, this smoke
borne here on fiery winds
at last stilled down.
So many last breaths, wild wishes
and long sorrows, brought to us,
transfigured in our misted air
our opal sea.

JO DEY

WIMMERA

Some journeys are not long enough.
Though I have travelled several days,
I have barely stroked the back
of this vast animal,
the long, bleached flanks,
the desiccated stubble of its hide.

I see the comfort that it needs
and its poor bones
that turn to powder.

How still it lies today,
hunkered down,
holding back its thirst
inside that thin and mangy skin.

Travellers on this land
ride behind their darkened windows.
To the moon, they are like ants
moving in haste, without purpose.

JO DEY

STRAW GUARDIAN

The lustrous air rustling by,
the boughs heavy with gold,
the thoughts filled with rich summer,
gold burning into being;
the world glowing with gold.

The nights blazing with brilliance,
spinning, never moving, never still,
liquid silver spilling
into the void, into the abyss,
into the nothingness.

The silvering,
the gold cascading, gone, never being,
the wheel rasping, the grasping frost;
the bonfire bright upon the hill,
the golden flare, the silver chill.

GEORGE WOOLMER

SO OLD THE DEEP WOODS

So old the deep woods, so older than we,
from far away days, each thicket and tree,
their trunks standing strong, true tempered by time,
aligned by wise nature's rhythm and rhyme.

Their old hollow limbs have lodged many guests,
who found in them comfort, and made there their nests;
and when the rains come and winds howl around,
there's always a place where they're safe and sound.

There's pleasantly spaced on branches and twigs,
fair leaves which a breeze sends dancing in jigs;
so let's steal away and let them all be,
and leave nature's grandeurs for others to see.

GEORGE WOOLMER

THE COCKIE'S COMPLAINT

I hate gum trees.
I loathe their dull green pendulous clumps
weeping for their dead brethren
I fear their hanging boughs
waiting on those still, quiet days
to make widows and orphans.

On soft spring mornings
I delight in the playful chatter
of maples and sycamores
the friendly hiss and distant roar
of the planted pinewoods
but the gum leaves tremble
whispering secrets
the ghost gum stands silently erect
a pale, impassive sentinel
while the she-oak moans softly
rustling her tattered skirts
in mournful misery.

I dread them on the hot, blasting days
I detest each grey twisted trunk
waving its withered arms
wagging its dead fingers
bone-dry, oil-rich tapers
begging for a match
to spark their shaggy crowns
into raging, vengeful beacons

When the summer is over
the gutters are glutted
with native leaf litter
that regularly tips
the precious rain
into wasteful waterfalls
and tints our baths
the colour of dried blood.

I stood outside last night, vowing
to cut down my hatred
and feed it to the woodstove
but instead I saw the moon above my head
reflected in a thousand silver scimitars
a constellation of earthbound stars
a forest of tiny lanterns signalling hope
and at last I loved that gum tree.

JULIA WAKEFIELD

MILLIPEDES

The year we separated
there was a plague
of millipedes
and our infestation
was the worst ever.
A neighbour said
the colour of our house
attracted them.

Each night I swept
the exterior clean
and by morning
the millipede army was back
tracking its way up
our pale rendered walls
leaving invisible trails
of toxin.

Their invertebrate bodies
like scars or scabs
often shaped into spirals
and question marks
and their thousand feathery legs
were like tiny sutures
that could not mend
our wounds.

SHARON KERNOT
Read at Salisbury Writers Festival, August 2009

TADPOLES

Fossicking for smooth stones at the water's edge
suddenly
I am eyeball to eyeball
with a smooth and polished frog:
the pulse in the hunched neck
throbs like the beat of my heart.

Now is the season when the first rush of winter
carries the dried flotsam and jetsam
away down the creek –
and the children rush after it,
carrying shiny jars and jam tins stripped of labels
and homemade fishing nets.

They plunge into the cold eddies capturing tadpoles.

They want to watch the strong back legs swell,
the little forelegs come out, the heads flatten
the tails disappear.

It is not long since they were tadpoles themselves –
swimming upstream
against the current.

Oh Lord!
I wish that I'd grown up to be a frog.

The world is too full of people
and not enough frogs.

BETTY COLLINS

CHRISTMAS BREAK

Elizabeth, a now-dowdy beauty,
rests on public holiday.
There's a break in court –
no parade of under-privilege today:
smoking away in the forecourt.
Time enough for summer's crimes.

There's a break in winter's drought:
the transplanted boabs settle
bloated like Christmas puddings.
Swollen by the sweet liquor
of rain.

A.M. SLADDIN

CHRISTMAS IN GAWLER

We pass the cave-glow
of a hundred front rooms,
to the place where a pine tree
lights the first star.

It's Christmas also down by the river,
where ice-cream van carols
pour into the darkness.

There, lit in two dimensions:
a fat Santa, frozen
in a bumpy ride
(kangaroos
instead of reindeer).

By popular demand,
Jesus and his manger
are off to one side.
An echidna, a wombat
and a platypus bring
their various gifts.

At least that's what
they're meant to be doing –
is it the joy of their delirium
that makes it look
so much like looting?

Anyway,
we liked it.

AIDAN COLEMAN

ON A MOONLESS NIGHT AT GRANGE

Tonight, the jetty has no end:
its wooden rails, bony arms outstretched,
vanish in darkness, sleepwalking west
across St Vincent Gulf.

I am here, at the city's edge, unmoored,
looking out to an invisible sea.
No distant flickering lights appear
on water or sky, no breeze touches skin,

no movement catches the eye.
The jetty is almost deserted:
only a lone fisherman dreams,
motionless beside his empty bucket.

I step out, feet sounding remote
on the boards, a narrow strip of bleached
wood unwinding. My body slows,
slips into the rhythm of the whoosh

and murmur of unseen waves.
I drift into sleep, walk sixty-five kilometres
along these weathered planks,
wake up on the shore of Yorke Peninsula.

DAVID ADÈS

SOMETHING LIKE EGYPT

A week or so after our arrival
I'm driving with my father
down Port Road to see the wharves
his large hands guiding the wheel
shirt sleeves rolled to his elbows
thinly rolled cigarette pasted to his lip.

It seems a hot day, though still winter
sun heating the cracked dashboard
red leather scent fusing this moment to memory
and row upon row of palm trees
planted on the wide median strip
convincing me we now belong
to an exotic and tropical country
something like Egypt.

DEB MATTHEWS-ZOTT
Read at Port Noarlunga, September 2009

BEACH FRENZY

at the beach
the wind gusts send

grainy sand
flying into faces

plastic buckets are blown
like feathers across the sand

beach balls lift up
& plonk down again into the sea

as seagulls circle
raucously above

debris skitters
along the promenade

bunting on the kiosk
whiplashes the air

cafe umbrellas
are quickly rolled

& plastic chairs pushed
under tables

people run for shelter
in a mass frenzy

while seemingly unaware
a Labrador dog paddles in the ocean

JILL GOWER
Winner – Imagist Poetry Competition 2009
Mentored Poet 2009

ANTIQUITY

Geese flying into the night;
Voices roaring in the wind
People from the north
People from the west
Across the water
Come the song
From the islands
From the rain country
And the mountains of fire
To the desert people
Night is coming
Hear the voices
The songs
Of Ujung Pandung and Melaka
Sing Lumad
Batak and Badjao
Through the forest
Over the sea
Voices crying in the wilderness
Whirlwind in the desert
The song goes on
I am antiquity
You will never destroy me!

DAVID BARKER
Read at Murray Bridge, September 2009

FORGOTTEN ROSES

Along a walkers' route,
    the Heysen Trail,
    ruins of a rural dwelling lie.
What's left of a chimney,
    the outlines of some walls
    are all that now remain.
Nearby another remnant lingers on:
    roses bloom in what had been a flowerbed,
    once nurtured by some woman's hand.
Unpruned, untended now,
    they do not spread
    but still they hold their own.
Were they a sign of love,
    proclaiming joy and affirmation,
    or but a forlorn substitute?
What happiness and hopes once flourished here,
    what sorrows and what griefs,
    what doings of their daily, yearly lives?

Did the family go away disaster-ridden,
    by misfortune crushed?
    Or did they move into a brighter future?
Long-forgotten human memories
    of human times and human feelings
    have sunk into a long-departed past.

Yet every year the roses still remember.

LAWRENCE JOHNSON

TREESOME

There is a tree where I go to
act, play and learn
(aren't all three the same?)

that's as old as Methuselah
looks comfortable in its space
though crooked-backed and bulbous

it has made its home, renovated,
cracking the surrounding pavement
while extending

I see it looking at me, eyes
everywhere, inviting a hug, a climb,
even love, unlike my father who

loved me while working hard
and gambling harder, unable to
hide his anger and fear

I haven't succumbed yet
but I will climb you, I will hug you
I do love you

PETER TSATSOULIS
Mentored Poet 2009

IN A HILLTOP HOLLOW

We lay there once
young
entwined
a diamond-sparked canopy
stretched
high above.

Our fire spent
content
we slept
sweet flowing waters
murmured.

Now I sit
aged
alone
a diamond-sparked canopy
stretched
high above.

No lulling water
murmurs
drying grass
rustles
in a fire-hot wind.

Yet
that long ago
is ever with me
giving strength
courage
patience.

I await the time
when
within the canopy
we will
once more embrace.

ELIZABETH BELL
Read at Murray Bridge, September 2009

SUMMER DREAM

I dreamed of the sun hanging
as red as earth in the morning sky.
It was the hottest summer ever.
Crows gathered in huge numbers
as if they were expecting something.

We slept under wet sheets, tossed and tangled
with dreams stacked on dreams like
animals in a children's story but atop
the rooster, a crow called its dire warning.

The grass dried and turned to tinder.
Trees fleshed themselves pure white.
Their tatters of bark clacked like rhythm sticks
in the relentless northerly wind.

In between we tossed in our sleep
dreamed of flame, of running immobile.
Great old trees died on the ridges
and stood, grey and bony.
Crows murdered there like huge black flowers.

In that season the sky was never blue.
Stars were hidden by dust and smoke
but towards morning the faintest breath
blew up from the south, carrying the scent
of something we remembered from long before,

something we wished for without knowing
what it was we wished for: the scent of rain.

BELINDA BROUGHTON

ONEIRIC

Of course, you know little of the fact that –
by night – I don a mask and moonlight,
alternately, as a prince and beggar. And
on other nights, as a Bengal tiger with flames
in place of claws. You do not see me firstly
as pure animal, then as pure machine.
The words alone – and the words must be alone –
are themselves the pearl of great price. And
I have made ready to sell all my belongings,
to set out into the field to dig the night.
Of course, you know little of the thousand dark,
wind-riven nights on which I was alone –
bruised, blundering through the field.
Blundering and yet gentle with the grasses:
folding each leaf down with measured caution.
Of course, you cannot know this –
you may only follow with telltale footsteps
through the darkness, unearthing reams
where you pass, where you fold them
down again. This is the dream. And the dream
from which you will waken. I will become
pure machine: lit from within by oil – golden oil,
oil of night. I will powder the field for treasure,
forgetting – perhaps – that the field itself
is priceless – the mother of all pearls.
I will blunder and yet be gentle, and yet
raise it up into darkness on flaming claws.

THOM SULLIVAN

THE CHANCE OF RAIN

Then there was nothing but breath: yours, mine
and the shallow, gasping rain.
That moment just after –
or was it before? –
time started flowing backwards.
We kissed.
My fingers surfed the ripples of your bare spine,
your bare skin against mine.
We undressed.
The last guests were leaving.
The party was in full swing.
You tasted of lime and sideways glances.
We kissed for the first time.
On the back porch, warm air and citronella smoke,
I took a chance, I took your hand.
You smiled and said hello.
I glanced down, suddenly self conscious.
There you were, pouring wine for a friend
and laughing and I wished I knew why.
An old song on the radio made me wonder if you'd be there.
That morning, I drank tea in my garden, alone,
looked at the clear sky, the brown grass,
thought to myself there was no chance of rain.

AMELIA WALKER

I THINK

about you with her.   think
through nights tumbled over flesh
whipped by this persistent affliction.
think with my guts
churning some bizarre fantasy and
fantasise about not
thinking.
think shallow pernicious
rumblings fed by misguided platitudes from friends
and lovers.
how long will
/ are you still
/ it won't last

so I run with sex and anarchy – we're
looking for faith
but can only find disbelief

                             mounting fear

we try to cut in
but it's a cold party – fear

                             an icy lay

I watch anarchy and stoned love flirting
with consummation, but they can't

                             keep it up

and nor could you, my love

my thinking is marred by my thoughts
I think

JENNY TOUNE
Mentored Poet 2009

COOKIES

Come and live with me
let's hold hands –

sure, we can't cope &
there'll be is no happy ending
but I don't care –

just come & live with me
we'll eat some cookies.

THEODORE W. SCHAPEL

LOVERS SLAIN

Ha! Taking a walk down
Lover's Lane . . .
I stopped
then laughed.
Me, I am taking a walk down
Lovers Slain

(corpses everywhere)

SARAH WAUCHOPE

HELLO, AT LAST

You asked me a question today
the first in six weeks,
you sat forward on your seat
put pen to paper
another first in six weeks

You had no snarl today
no aggro pouring out
of those pimples
on your cheeks

I saw how clear is the blue
of your eyes now
and I knew
your smile
would be worth the wait

SARAH WAUCHOPE

OPTIMISTIC FOR OPTIMISM

Behind every cumulus cloud
a bright light shines warm
casting its rays over space
that to our knowledge is limitless.
Presenting to me here on earth
the idea that if space can exist
without a predetermined end
so can I.
I now try to consider space
in my present and potential actions
for I too am unlimited
and, with the right momentum
I shall never stop.
                    – Nanette age 14

ANDREW ELLERY

THE LEMON TREE

There was a lemon tree
my father planted

unwisely
in a sea of couch

He did things like that
If it's tough enough, it'll live!

I'd sneak out at night
to keep those grass fingers
from gripping its throat

I'd put rose petals on its feet
make the fairies dance around it
polish the leaves – persistently

Still it curled its green leather
pretended not to care

i sung it as though i were Arrernte *
i sung it like it belonged
and the grass did not

Two years it lived
whistling that old
failure-to-thrive tune

In the final spring it gave one
porcelain flower
which swelled into

a green fruit that
died before it could
grow fat and yellow

My father pulled it up like a twig
threw it into the incinerator

I found that lemon
hard and indestructible
in the ashes the next day

so I saved it
for this poem
and all the others.

CARMEL WILLIAMS
Read at Salisbury Writers Festival, August 2009

(Arrernte: indigenous people of the Alice Springs region)

HER INDOORS

She sits in the quiet of night
listening for the special tone of silence
that heralds his presence
he is with her as she segues
from day to night
imperceptibly caressing her shoulders
as they heave with as yet unshed tears
he is curled around her feet
a phantom cat paying homage to her stillness
as she folds herself into bed
he blows in her ear and nibbles at the edges of her mind
through her luscious, busy sleep
he is there ... never stepping into her dreams
just calmly standing by, bearing witness
and when she wakes, awash in images and fears and worries
she tastes him in her coffee
and lets him settle on the back of her palate
she puts on her clothes, some dirty from yesterday
but always clean knickers,
with him tucked under the elastic
like a child's hanky from her school days
her handbag is cluttered with the stuff of her day –
wallet, keys, gym pass, five lipsticks, her love for him –
slung across her overloaded shoulders
as she heads out the door
to an uncertain future.

TRACEY KORSTEN

LOST

Observing kitchen window lost
chasing thoughts amongst the frost
for what awaits through misted glass
soon to be tomorrows past

Scratched and smeared all but broken
dusts from pasts have been awoken
a flower seen bruised from a child
outside the world can be quite wild

In gentle breath you write your name
or whisper sorry in the rain
blow a bubble while washing dishes
a chicken bone rests for making wishes

As sunlight warms the battered pane
tear like streaks will form again
as droplets dance upon the sill
revive a violet lying still

JACQUELINE KIMBER
Read at Murray Bridge, September 2009

LOVE AND FEAR

The language of love
is intercepted by
the language of fear
skittering around the edges
of isolation
separating
spirit knowledge
in mutual antagonism
of strife infested conflicts
where self-interest barricades
itself with the armour of
fear.

The language of fear
is penetrated by
the language of love
embracing all the spaces
of loneliness
enfolding
higher ideals
in mutual recognition
of truth infected encounters
where selflessness invites
unity of positive action
love.

MAEVE ARCHIBALD

GRACE'S RAINBOW

Dear Grace,
child of imagination and lightness of heart,
you painted me a rainbow of true colours
to keep in my kitchen gallery
of grandchildren's art.

When a strong, bright rainbow
stretched across the afternoon sky
above the garden's red autumn roses
on your birthday party day with friends,
you exclaimed in joy,
The rainbow is my best present.

May you always know
such joy and hope.

DAWN COLSEY

WALKING GRACE TO SCHOOL
at 5½ years old

Can I keep this feather. Isn't it beautiful?
She holds the magpie's gift,
caresses the soft tufts near the quill.
You can, I tell her, wondering why she doubts,
her mother fanatical for keeping clean.

Every angel has white feathery wings –
her next pronouncement.
I've never seen one, I venture.
Oh, they all do, with total assurance.

She skips ahead, chanting her morning song,
Run, run, as fast as you can.
Can't catch me, I'm the gingerbread man.
Come on, Granny. Come on.
I check her little shoulders.
No feathers.
But still, an angel.

DAWN COLSEY

AT LUNCH

My mother
is almost twice as old
as my father was
when he died.

She
is only half aware
that when I am with her
I am doubly bad tempered.

My mother
can increase my feelings of inadequacy
twofold
and halve my self-esteem.

But
at lunch
my mother and I
share a baguette
and a serviette
and a strawberry tart.

We jointly buy
crossword scratchies
and share the winnings
if there are any

and when my wine glass
is half empty
she fills it up
from her own.

JUDY DALLY

THE LITTLE YELLOW PLANE

It's just a little yellow plane
with two wings and a splash of glue.
It's the same one
my father left me
in nineteen-sixty-four.

I was just five
when he was changed into a number
resting peacefully in a wheat paddock
growing the road toll.

In my hand this
miniature cloud-buster
soars no further
than to the horizon
at the end of my arm.

Yet my memories of him
showing off that tiny machine
easily wing across the vastness
of the forty-four years.

He has always been on my radar
always been my co-pilot
tapping the compass
my wingman watching my back.

I just wish
he could descend from the heavens
so we could go flying together.

GARY MACRAE
Read at Salisbury Writers Festival, August 2009

JUDITH

We came to expect it of her
but it still astonished us –
her noticing of need
and her quickness to see
what she could do to meet it.
What we saw in her,
in that alien and confronting environment,
was an instinct for empathy,
a compassion reflex,
fluency in the language of acceptance,
a grasp of the grammar
of the spontaneous act of kindness.

In Varanasi, rugged up
against the pre-dawn chill,
we stepped ashore
after a boat ride on the Ganges
viewing the ghats.
When she saw the oarsman rub his hands,
it seemed to her his need
was greater than hers
and on impulse she turned back,
reached across language,
culture, race, religion
and gave him her gloves.
And because she was tall
and he was slim,
and because she was human
and had seen that he was too,
the gloves fitted.

JOHN PFITZNER

SCARVED WOMEN

cuddle newborn loaves
to their breasts

weave wide skirts
through potato
and onion sacks

lettuce head girls
arrange
fresh picked flowers

embroider dreams
with sun thread laughter

LIDIJA ŠIMKUTĖ

AFTER CASSANDRA

Yet on we strove unmindful, deaf and blind,
To place the monster on our blessed height.
                    (The Aeneid: Virgil 2.234–9)

The gods have granted us a special gift
in that we cannot tell what is to come.
For truth from error we can barely sift –
unlike Cassandra, grateful to be dumb,

unable to give warning to a friend,
for prescience might bring despair:
if cursed by seeing where their acts might tend,
such knowledge of the future we'd not bear.

So like the Trojans we bring monsters in;
we welcome those who lead to doom.
Unable to distinguish good from sin,
we fail to see the worm inside the bloom.

Incapable of knowing, see us smile and nod
and welcome in a devil whom we think a god.

VALERIE VOLK
Winner – John Bray Roman Poetry Prize, 2009

YIA YIA'S APPROVAL

Yia Yia's approval
is conditional
on sitting still
quietly
keeping your jumper on
cold or not
deferring to her assessment
of the weather
eating not too much
not too little
washing your hands after touching
anything
not touching anything she thinks
should not be touched
speaking clearly
in English or in Greek
none of which you do with ease
if at all.

She has no pet name for you
your sister is Koukla
your cousin Loulouthi
you are greedy
naughty.
It's not that she doesn't love you
I see this, as you sit together easily
cross-legged on the verandah
silently exchanging smiles
cracking walnuts from her tree.

KATE ALDER
Mentored Poet 2009

WILD MOTHER CAT

I met you knitting for charity
such fierce protectiveness coming from you
such determination
such a stake on life
you won't let go
sixty-eight years of life and sparking with energy

I see the core of struggle in you
the marks of the abusive marriage
violence to you and your children
you got out
fighting!

I see that protectiveness, Wild Mother Cat
I see the scars where you fought for your freedom
I see the scratch marks in the earth around you
as you defy anyone to imprison you ever again
your tattered ears, your well used claws
the scars across your face and body
the pain that drove you
the protectiveness that gave you fire
Wild Mother Cat who now knits for charity
grows Trees for Life
takes Meals on Wheels to those with less than you

Your grandchildren have not grown up with the destruction
your children were forced to endure

Wild Grandmother Cat may you live long
may you revel in the satisfaction that you are no longer powerless
    to protect
know the satisfaction that no one within your circle will see that
    abuse again
know the satisfaction that never again will you be required to watch

Long life to you
fierce protectress
Wild Grandmother Cat.

SUZANNE REECE
Mentored Poet 2009

PHILIPPINO GREENS

I hobble into the consulting room.
Dr Vier pontificates,
You have rheumatoid arthritis.
You need steroid treatment.
Injections.
Let's get on top of it quickly.
I hesitate.
It must be diet related,
I insist.

Dr Vier leans back, puts fingertips together,
looks self-satisfied and reflects,
No, it's nothing to do with what you eat.
Although . . .
Cousin Mervyn was bed-ridden with what you've got,
ate nothing but greens for three months,
got himself up,
divorced his partner who'd walked out,
went off to the Philippines,
made a new marriage
and was never heard of again.

I consider my options.

ALICE SHORE
Read at Salisbury Writers Festival, August 2009

DOWNSIDE OF JARGON

Correct your wrong thinking? Huh!
Select jargon when pleaded.
Correct your bad bonding? Huh!
Deed by thought is preceded.

Trial association with white coats
So doctors feel information blocks
Have their manipulative theories tested
With 'psychotic', 'compulsive neurotic' and ECG Shocks.

However strange, caring and devious,
Every belief in language is spoken,
We invented the words, invented the Gods,
Are we to use these only as tokens?

From high Taj Mahal to nature's low craters
Tongues in grief select dust to dust
Honour the language of marital law
On funeral pyres. The 'trust' becomes 'must'.

When action speaks for itself
And no words are needed
Inspiration, deception and concept
Nevertheless – are heard, seen and heeded.

LORNA DWYER

THE AUNT'S STORY

We used to say
*You'll make it
to one hundred auntie!*
and she would
roll her eyes
and moan
I'm tired.

She almost
completed the sentence.
Curled against
white pillows
like a comma
before the last
full stop.

JUDY DALLY

THE GOLDEN JOURNEY
on visiting an exhibition of Japanese art at the Art Gallery of South Australia

coffee outside
she seeks the sun's warmth
while I avoid it
she eats cake since
her cancer came back

young at fifty
we are new grandmothers
sharing photos
she says she just wants
to see him grow up

in the gallery
old Shinto gods
greet us
we talk about everything
but

this Buddha's
non-grasping face
fades with age
the gallery's care lavished
on not letting it go

art about
the Four Noble Truths
but I desire
long life and happiness
for my friend

a small ivory
of a boy hitting a drum
being time
here is your grandson
I say and she smiles

BELINDA BROUGHTON
Winner – Tanka Sequence: Japanese Poetry Competition 2009

VISITING HOURS

I considered grapes for this friend
who, prone in white, stares with awe
at something beyond my shoulder –
yet offer only clichés by card and tongue
to avoid the thorns in unguarded greetings.

I share the burden of his dry leaf whisper
as we talk about his visitors, trivia of later life,
even sport, anything except the graph
that stutters across his clipboard
to haunt those memories we always rearrange,
but today falter, too soon
leave a silence barren as dead twigs.

Wish I'd brought those grapes.

DAVID COOKSON
Read at Port Noarlunga, September 2009

FIRES

As the hills burn
the cancer ward
affords you
a fireproof bunker;
but embers
have crept
under your skin
and the flames
are consuming you
from within.

JUDY DALLY

RETURN FROM HOSPITAL

I have not crossed mountains to be here
but merely continued
to breathe

guided only by the stars
of a few machines
and the fact
of you

sometimes
I didn't know you

(a brick
where the praying-heart
should be)

but now in the quiet
we make each evening

I find I don't believe
in death

the psalm unfolds its rivers
and hills

I'm
delivered

unbroken

to sleep or love

AIDAN COLEMAN

PROPRIETY

At night Gran kept her teeth
in a glass above the bathroom basin
where I washed my face before I went to bed.
I'll eat you in your sleep, they snarled.

Gran and Gramps were old but still alive.
They sat and ate their meals with us and
Gran used butter knives, napkins and said grace.
Gramp's yellow moustache strained his tea,
Gran's false teeth chomped and ground
and food stuck in, especially green Brussel sprouts.

Gran died. All puffed and white, they dressed her
in the lavender *crepe de chine* she wore for best.
Gramps cried. He polished her black shoes then
the undertaker put them on her tiny feet.
They laid her on my parents' front room double bed.

The adults made me look at her. She seemed
asleep and empty but her teeth were in.
I wondered had they glued them in her mouth
to make them stick so she'd look alright
for when she went to heaven.

TESS DRIVER

THE VISIT

She is at my door
her six-week-old baby
asleep on her shoulder.

She has come to
introduce her treasure
to her ageing neighbour

a neighbour unused to
cradling a sleeping child
in her arms.

Watching that tiny face
eyes shut, mouth closed
fingers relaxed

I recall an old man
his voice quivering
saying sorry to us

for the world
his generation was
passing on.

ERICA JOLLY

UNBORN

The kick of you
strong as a hatchling on Turtle Island
                            making for the sea
Swimming already
in a quiet womb sea
where the tide is a pulse
shhhh shhhh shhhh shhhh

The roll and tumble, the wiggle and stretch of you
the immediacy, the wilfulness and sureness of you

The punch of you
punching in belly all your announcements
                                speaking without voice

Saying *I am here* and
watch me grow and
open the door and
me me me me.

DAVID ADÈS

SHEETS

Starched, white and stainless,
morning ghosts of last night's lust,
chastened by the sun,
pinned by pursing wooden lips,
silencing the neighbour's tongue.

MARIA VOUIS

TOWELS

tumbling together
remind me of you

G.M. WALKER

THE BELLY OF THE POT

When I fell for him
it was in the pub
the first night we met.
There was a pot there,
a small red glazed urn
and he talked in his
curious accent about the
belly of the pot and
traced the back of his
index finger over it
as if it was a real belly
or a breast. That was it.
Of course I ended up
in his bed and after
some years was bearing
a belly like that pot:
his daughter. And now
she is bearing a belly
like that pot and I'm
still angry that he got
sick at all, let alone
died, even though he
was a shit. I would
have liked her father
to watch her swelling.

BELINDA BROUGHTON

APOLLO'S TENTH

She's subtle – inconspicuous – just as
a central sentence or a lion's den.
But, being notes and never cents, she sends
away loose change / pursues a lonesome strange:
and in her modern independence, she's
a moment's movement, moment by moment;
and when she moves, she beats her body out
for Apollo in rhythm and rhyme that
rights our poppy ghetto; but she's nervous
– a toe ahead of tomorrows; untamed.
Terribly adorable and inverse
to Heavenly Muse, she's written down; toyed with
yet always toying – she's muse of art
appreciation.
             Touched by you, she's soft
to the skin as whispers might be; her body
a cool breeze to your dry and dusty eye.
And though it's too oft difficult to see,
she's full-feathered in secret choruses
and completes the poet's verse, having what's hers
when songs aren't left unsung and hymns unheard.

PEACH HOWEY-LENIXXH

CARBORUNDUM VITAE

Deep within the forests
lie the seams of coal
dark, dirty, dusty stuff
the stuff of nightmares
of industrial behemoths
the stuff that runs the
dark, satanic mills
bequeathed to us by our ancestors
mysterious, murky, majestic

And here I stand
my Davey Lamp lighting the way
listening always for the canary's song
hoping still for a diamond,

yet knowing that the coal must come first.

TRACEY KORSTEN

ROOMS OF DISCOVERY

there he is
a moss covered rock
amongst the roses

pulling weeds and
pruning the dead wood
lost in the aroma of life

he lets his garden ramble
in rooms of discovery
then gently shapes for light

HEATHER SLADDIN-STUART

STARS
for Luke

your hands have become
weapons to plunge

through the wire
that was framed & welded

to protect you from what is at
the end of the garden path

at night on the back step your mother sits
& stares into her father's yard

three generations under one roof
the absent husband, father, son in law

& you, son, still pounding
holes in the sky for stars to fill

RORY HARRIS

SIDEWAYS

His brain functions superbly with shapes and numbers.
At four, in church during the sermon, he drew from memory
an Egyptian mummy, with miniature mummies inside her,
in perfect symmetry; and Darth Vader of menacing stance
bursting with technology – each phase intense,
lasting months, even years –
pirates, archaeology, police vans.

But he can't piece together the jigsaw of people;
at school he's taken to kissing other children on the lips –
videos show this is the way to give and get love.
Little girls are surprised, parents recoil with horror,
a hostile father accosts the boy's mother, who then
instructs him clearly
Don't touch anyone
Next day after school, stiffening, she says casually,
How did it go today?
Alright he said *I didn't touch anyone*
but it was hard with my bag in the corridor
going sideways.

ROS SCHULZ
Poem of the Month, August 2009
Mentored Poet 2009

TRY TO BUTTON

you are old & have lost
your marbles, you gave up

walking years ago, but now
outside in the facility's garden

slouched in your princess chair
a brush of early autumn

across your face
you raise a couple of hands

& try to button the open collar
to turn the chill from your neck

as you would have done
all those years ago

along the high street
a British soldier on your arm

Ulster during the War
but before your troubles

RORY HARRIS

TRANSCENDENCE

two weeks ago in japan i sat on that Mountain
the bald young monk explaining zazen meditation
the release from past and future
and the silence of engyoji temple
teaching me the here/now
and here and now we sit in The Vales
a silence broken
by the eternal happiness of hi-5
on a blaring tv
which is everlasting
you my balding father
hair stolen not by time but radiation
you sit on the bed in your tracksuit pants
bulging with the incontinence nappy
below your buddha belly
your corporeal form shapeless as a toddler's
i ask if you need anything
you don't
all your physical needs met
in this daily malignant shallowness
the blastoma has excised your past
and your future is inoperable
you don't remember who came yesterday
or what you ate for breakfast
you have achieved a kind of benign transcendence
only those around you
feel the eternal depths of sorrow
but you
are in the perpetual
Here and Now.

ROB WALKER

TO CONFORM

Caught like a fly
in a spider web
restless to be free
senselessly we struggle
against our restraints
against society

Deprived of thought
of our imagination
we flounder
amongst the oppressive
unable to blossom
we wilt

Our resolve shattered
torn from the breast
a pitiful sight
is the listless being
the empty shell
society has left

LYNETTE ZANDER
Read at Murray Bridge, September 2009

RIDING ON A BLEAK TRAIN OF THOUGHT

Setting my sights on you in the night train,
riding along on a bleak train of thought.
my resistances crumble like rocks from a siding.
the tracks say my name to the serious night.
      They're calling me on, calling me strong.

Evil knows evil and knows where to find it,
the music turns nasty and dancing's macabre.
slamming our bodies to the beat of the carriage
i open the window and then you are gone.
      i don't hear you cry, you don't hear me sigh.

Darkness does not come only at night time,
it's here all the time in corruption and lies.
arrogance alibis nothing but destruction . . .
reconcile your sins before you step on.
      i may not be far, from where you are.

KERRYN TREDREA

TRAINS OF THOUGHT

Trains of thought have no timetables
nor, if they did,
would they keep to schedule.

Trains of thought almost always pull in
when you
are busy doing something else.

It is best to travel lightly on a train
of thought leaving
mobiles and iPods stowed at the station.

Though they may have many carriages
all, except the one
you're in, are completely empty.

Trains of thought run on the fuel
of pure Imagination
of which there are endless reserves.

When delivered to your platform
disembark quickly before
the train runs away with your thoughts.

JOHN MALONE
Read at Port Noarlunga, September 2009

THE REFUSAL

the refusal of domesticity, of mundanity,
TV, plasma, order and chaos,
letterbox drops and charge cards . . .

the refusal of Devonshire, lollypops,
foil wrapped, baked not fried,
sugar dusting, fuel, lies and other
gob-stopping, blocking acid treats;

fortunes and fate, failure, success and mediocrity,
nakidity and cloth, religion, day to day,
omnipresence, dizziness and apathy . . .

the refusal to split, and drive, keep inside the edges,
grow lawn, kill lawn, be forlorn or against,
of indecision and un-surity . . .

The refusal of acquisition and emptiness,
of day beds, and washing lines, traffic fines,
black and white, grey matter,
all matter, of time . . .

the refusal . . . keeps me alive.

the refusal . . . keeps me alive.

INDIGO

IN SIGNIFICANCE

In significance
    the stare of the world unnerves
    stars re-sculpt themselves
    ever thinner / brighter / lighter
    ever more dazzling
    'til they're pared to oblivion.

In significance
    little secrets become worldwide
    self-serving fingers know
    all the weak points.
    Doctor never knows any better.

In significance
    ever, unrest: lashed at fame's mast
    by envy's snickering tongue.

Even after death
    the bald truth will out.
So, though I have my own petty ambitions
    they quail under
    my store of gossip's munitions.

Sometimes
    I thank my insignificance.

A.M. SLADDIN

IT'S US WHO REMAIN

Out where the edge of town meets the scrub,
Bitumen turns then straightens up,
There's an old tree watching, taking its toll,
On anyone passing out of control.

Where nature strips bare, lives are reduced,
Bark scarred and twisted, scavengers roost,
Where flowers are sun-dried, visitors loiter,
Siblings and parents, teary-eyed suitors.

The knots and the scars of that tree are all ours,
We pass by so quickly like springtime and flowers,
In time we may heal, but our love still remains,
A scent, an aroma engraved in our veins,
Engraved in our veins.

Out where the edge of town meets the scrub,
Bitumen turns then straightens up,
There's an old tree watching, taking its toll,
On anyone passing out of control,

Old tree watching, old tree watching
What's over in seconds, lasts for a lifetime,
It's us who remain need a lifeline.

CLAYTON WERNER

CAUGHT RED-FACED

The officer pulls my car over
How can I help you? I ask
You've just crashed into two cars
T-boned one and had a head-on with another
I'm taking you into custody
But constable, I say, *this is the sideshow*
we are driving dodgem cars
Oh, he says, red-faced
In that case, I'll let you off with a warning.

DANE NIELSEN

BOTTLE

He heaves himself
as a seemingly empty
bottle into the clatter
and clank of the north
tide to join other
suitably dressed bottles
in the evening current
along Currie Street
and tributaries
past café and barber shop
shoe repairer
and dry cleaning stop
through the rapids
and into the mouth
of railway station
where the eddied swirl
of long neck stubby
frosted clear clouded
and coppered
washes into crated rattle
of journey home

GAETANO AIELLO

SALVATION ARMY HOSTEL

each morning
on the steps
of the Salvation Army hostel

a chemically troubled
woman sits

her street tan
is the colour of terracotta
and hair the texture of hessian

in the nerve-end
of her
stare

the dull pulse
of the peak hour traffic
unravels
itself

with a cigarette
behind each ear
and one in her hand

she waits as calmly
as a getaway car

JULES LEIGH KOCH

CHRISTINE'S BREAKFAST

After Prozac
a coffee

and two cigarettes
her senses are hot-wired

while the sunlight through
her window

is no longer
a foreign language

nor is its warmth
displaced

for now
her thoughts have taken

Pterodactyl
w i n g s

JULES LEIGH KOCH

DES RES

A teenaged girl then, maybe fifteen,
hormone-packed, hot, wanting
to be wanton – she knew more
than the lustiest courtesan,

the busiest prostitute, more
than a child should know. Older now,
she knows she knew nothing. Sex
is not the key to happiness.

It opens a door, but not to any room
she might want to live in. Not
the door to love and life, but a door
to darkness, no warmth or solace,

no comfort or ease; a space where men
offer much but leave a bitter taste,
a feeling of fear and a fear of feeling.
They call her from that dark place,

praising her and the sordid cell
where illusions of love and life dwell,
illusions that magically turn
from shining hope to sordid pain

with a word and a finger snap.
She learns to scratch the surface,
detect the lies below the gilt, the fake
magic that could snap her in half

and leave her crushed and weeping.
She learns to inspect spaces on offer,
have them surveyed, and finally
she learns to refuse anything

that doesn't meet her standards.

CAROLYN CORDON
Read at Salisbury Writers Festival, August 2009

'MY POOR FOOL'

'Prometheus was a fool'
Avalanche, after Aeschylus

I love fools
fools on the hill
fools, like Grock,
bringing the sorrows
of the nineteen thirties
into the circus ring.

I love fools
feel the strength
in their fragility
take in the truths
they dare to speak
truths that cost their lives.

ERICA JOLLY

NOT GOAT BUT SHEEP

Eamon found the line to God
at school, with catechisms
shoved down his throat
until he could spew them up
all over unbelievers, so
the words stuck to their less
than heavenly raiment. Stuck
so hard only harsh scrubbing
would remove the words.

The alcohol didn't help, or
maybe drink brought the whole
thing on. Be careful owning up
to godless ways to an Irish sailor
a long, long way from home.
It ended well enough – the
unbeliever thinking hard all the
drive home, and the Catholic boy
happy to have gathered
a wayward sheep for God.

CAROLYN CORDON
Read at Salisbury Writers Festival, August 2009

PASSAGES
Australian War Memorial, Canberra.

Two colonnades
long porticos, their
facings open arches
silent sentries.
Face to face
two halls with walls
streaked red with blood
'til walking close
what seemed as this
but ruby flowers
'midst laddered rows.
Laddered rows
like cresting waves
or furrowed dirt
where crimson grows
from fallen seeds,
their naming
in remembrance
entrance
into memory's flood.

GENNY DREW
Poem of the Month, March 2009

STEPPING OUT

National Museum of the American Indian, New York.

Thirty pairs of moccasins
are advancing in a ring, stepping out
in a spiral from the centre
where slippers made to wrap around
a child's first steps are glad with beads
and braids and coloured threads.
The moccasins grow longer and larger
until further on around the ring
well-worn shoes tipped with porcupine quills
are moseying along.
As if to escape the museum floor
they glide away in single file
following the memory
of a beating drum, wild cries
and the rank smell and frenzied rush
of herds of driven buffalo.
As though after a powwow
this company of moccasins is pressing
forward and outward and on.

ELAINE BARKER

END OF HOSTILITIES

when i
have lost
as much
as gained
my pain
and whittled
circumstance
dictate i
stow my
gun and
sheath its
bayonet
with a
promise
not to
scorch
the earth
behind me
as i
leave

ALAN P. KELLY
Read at the Port Adelaide Festival, October 2009

MUTTON BIRDS, ANZAC DAY

You have only two instructions:
should you become disoriented,
do your best to find your bearings,
then head north as planned;
when things get rough,
remember, hold your nerve,
and keep low at all costs.

IAN GIBBINS

SHIELDS

You say they hide
themselves behind
civilians as
human shields.

When you shell
a hospital
with phosphorous
that burns the structure
and the skin
around the wounded,
and when you shell
a school where people
flee for refuge
where are the shields?

And when you fire
your guided rockets
at the homes
of target persons,
sometimes with luck
you find them home
but surely slay
his wife and children.
Does a man hide
when he's at home?

No whitewash words
paint thick enough
to hide your evil.
Murder is murder
whatever the wrapping.

MURRAY ALFREDSON
Joint Winner – Political Poetry Competition 2009

ANTS

Bits of flesh in their mouths . . .
cheering and thrilling . . .
they are running, shoulder to shoulder,
in rows, in lines, marching peelpeel peelpeel . . .

Crossing verandah . . .
climbing up walls
towards an unknown tunnel
in rows, in lines, marching peelpeel peelpeel . . .

 A crow died yesterday . . .
no trace of it is left now . . .
and crows have gathered from ten countries
in rows, in lines, marching peelpeel peelpeel . . .

Draught blown by wings . . .
kahkah kahkah by the drumming beaks . . .
and lumps in their mouths
in rows, in lines, marching peelpeel peelpeel . . .

They are running in an unending flow . . .
cheering and thrilling . . .
a battalion of ants
in rows, in lines, marching peelpeel peelpeel . . .

PRITHVINDRA CHAKRAVARTI
Read at Port Noarlunga, September 2009

THE MATHEMATICS OF POVERTY

The poor keep moving
as if relocation
could reframe the algebra.

They cannot see that repetition
traces patterns
in their life.

New beginnings become as hopeless
as stale finales
of debt and desperation.

Wishful thinking makes for certainties
gambling against the odds
of possibilities.

Whispered prayers and incantations
leaves no space
for reason's compass to steady and settle.

If they stood still and mapped the moment
both sides of the equation
would simplify

and they might construct
a new geometry
of anger.

M.L. EMMETT

GRAPHS

Look at graphs,
see playful colours dance
across
bureaucratic grids
of black
and white.

Know percentages,
see numbers
rise
or fall,
measuring,
weighing
global poverty
– and compassion.

Watch breaths
catch
in well-padded throats
adorned
with golden crosses.

Then,
present more
graphs . . .

YR HAM

ART VS SCIENCE

Science tells us we are monkeys
clinging tenuously to life
on a thin, dying crust
surrounding roiling molten rock
which is surrounded in turn
by a mostly toxic air bubble
all of which is hurtling through space
towards the big whimper.

Art is the strategy we employ
to distract us from these facts.

God is the hope that
it's all just a horrible dream
that we will wake on fresh sheets
to the smell of coffee brewing
and have nowhere particular to go.

ROB HARDY

WORLD NOISE DAILY
(Cee En En On-line, Page 1)

Our failure, which art our haven
Let us laud it in *Breaking News*:
copycat massacres, billion dollar bailouts
malfunctioning rockets and poisoned baby food

Our *Guardian*, which art our foundation
Let us ignore the nuclear standoff
enemies of Israel and the African crisis
to focus on that stuntman stuffed into a dryer

Our *News-Dot-Com*, which art our daily read
Let us keep our faces poker
over *Old man runs Ice ring; Minister smoked dope*
and *Dad finds porn on teenager's phone*

Our future, which art in havoc
Let's choke in methane but keep growing beef;
fill the Pacific with plastic waste;
replace the trees with nuclear cities;
then shoot off to the first station in Space.

JANINE BAKER
Joint Winner – Political Poetry Competition 2009

ALL HAIL THE ILLOGICAL INFERENCE

A President who reads poetry –
a *non sequitur* perhaps
like the undertaker who loves life
or the masochist who laughs at her own jokes.

Miller Williams, poet, read for President Clinton –
did Prime Minister Rudd select a poet?
(Les Murray? No, not a Party man);
perhaps a 'sleeping line' from Peter Porter?

Robert Frost wrote for President JFK,
read for him his poem 'The Gift Outright'.
Elizabeth Alexander read her poem for victorious Obama –
at his request. A President who carries
verse beneath his arm.

Australian poets' verses collect the dust
while politicians spin spineless epithets
and Tall Poppies' bones crunch
beneath Dame Edna's size twelve shoes.

TESS DRIVER

TO THE ONE WHO RIDES THE RAINBOW

Indigo,
when you compose
cosmological verse,
the aesthetic heart of the universe
shifts its fickle ground –
inner and inner, deeper and deeper,
more and more profound.

Beauty moves its nucleus
from smell to taste to touch to sight
and then to sound, and then to far beyond,
to the subtlest edge to which a mind can stretch.

Just as nebulae condense into a star,
and beauty of form begins to appear,
your message of light and delightful style
give form to sublime idea.

You paint beguiling stars with a palette of femininity.
Above the senses you build a bridge to connect with infinity.
You consecrate the page with your concept of divinity.
Spangling gems you cut and set in the heart of our community.
Ringing with purity, they clang a bell
whose echoes climb
the stairwell of my spine
until they reach the landing beyond all understanding,
where they roar like a boundless ocean's massive swell –
as big a bang as any with which creativity can explode!
I call upon every friend who in this street does dwell
to study your aesthetic mode.
If only we all were blessed with your poetic stance,
every soiree of poesy would surely end in cosmic trance.

KALICHARAN NIGEL DEY

PREPARATION FOR AN INTERVIEW

Drink the better part
of a bottle of red

tell yourself again
you want the job

watch the late news
& before David Letterman

read through once more
your career highlights

anticipate the questions
& when you're in there

hope they don't notice
evidence of the wine

you've read up
on the latest techniques

& won't be deterred
by emotionless responses

though you do your best to read
the subliminal signs

such as the cold handshake
from the Chair

who breaks eye contact
a moment too soon as you leave

& two weeks later
you take that call

an exceptionally high quality field
please apply again in future

like the interview questions
the feedback begins to sound the same

you hang up the phone
& bask in a familiar sense of relief

you read the same news
on half a dozen papers online

you check the office emails
you check your gmail, twitter & facebook

you check the news again
soon it's coffee time

only another three hours to go
    there must be something else . . .

STEVE BROCK

OVERWRITING

Write over the top of this. Write
across the surface of dried ink and wood pulp.

Over clumps of curves and lines
and the sharp edges of serifs. As if words

would die without breath in their lungs.
Write as if each sequence of letters

shapes the landscape of language.
Inscribe your name in the margins.

Rearrange the furniture of a sentence.
Enjamb phrases in unexpected

places. Insert or delete a stanza.
Stretch or shrink lines. Create

a caesura. Widen gaps. Amplify
silences. Note the beauty

of blank space, then leave this page
for others to write over.

Let it transform into something
unimagined, a body that curls

and rises under the warm
flesh of a stranger's fingertips.

CAMERON FULLER

AT WRITERS WEEK OPENING DAY

A thousand people (intellectuals all)
sitting on the lawn, at Writers Week
intent on the Premier (in the tent)
Mike Rann Himself
telling us about how
he's ALWAYS been
SO enlightened
about Aborigines
acknowledged we're on Kaurna land –
(not one obviously aboriginal person in the crowd though) –
suddenly from behind, up on the path,
a loud yell:
Oi!
Everyone turns to see
an obviously angry, obviously Aboriginal man –
(he's probably drunk) –
the crowd embarrassed
hope he'll go away.

He yells again, I think what he says is
Oi! Liar!

Then to everyone's relief
he does go away.

The chasm
remains.

BRUCE BILNEY

CONFESSION

i am not a poet
i am a borrower
in the library of books
that crumble when opened
and sigh when closed

i am not a poet
i am a thief
in the house of meanings
written in invisible ink
in unknown languages

i am not a poet
i am a supplanter
in the matrix of ideas
that always were
and always will be

i am not a poet
and this is not a poem

MARK C. MARTIN

GLASS

i opened a book
and all the words fell out
they litter the ground at my feet
crunching underfoot
like broken glass

my kingdom for a pair of shoes

MARK C. MARTIN

I AM THE MOMENT
with thanks to Tess

I am the moment between
the words and punctuation

Where conversation stops
there I remain hidden

Through speech I am disrobed –
I am the moment that is forgotten.

THEODORE W. SCHAPEL

THIS FEELING

Is it fear loneliness fear of loneliness surrendered voice lack of
voice sold words drifting hope lack of concrete evidence? is it
rough soil hard terrain crumbling footings deep tracks heavy
boulders lost shoes too far to travel? is it soft skies hard edges
sunny sides down cracked blankets low clouds fast sunsets torn
threads thrown-in cushions? is it sharply stated under felt loosely
joined irretrievably catalogued limply labelled? is it clearly turbulent
waving backwards neatly expensive forgiving fraudulent sorry for
the right things? is it floating downhill closing doorways badly
painted mispronounced faith hovering higher than grappling palms?
is it?

INDIGO

THE TRUTH OF TEARS

Do you ever want to be somebody else,
to go back to the day before yesterday?
Archaeologists are taught
that the sides of an excavation
are more important than the bottom
but there are times when I want to go back
and start the dig all over again.

Life is sometimes a slippery slope,
error begetting error, out of control,
like a mud slide after torrential rain.
Lose your footing and you end up
arse-up at the bottom of the heap,
muddied, tearful and confused.

Family are often no help at all
their long tongues prying and prodding at
the broken tooth of your inner hurt.
Have you noticed how almost everyone
likes to have a lick at the salty stuff
which spills from other people's souls.

Sodium chloride slowly gnaws away
and even the strongest anchor and chain
turns red in the jaws of a cruel sea.
But salt is also a preservative
and sometimes we need to weep salt tears
to preserve what sanity we have.

MARY BRADLEY

HOPE

Green rose buds
promise pink petals –
aphids like jewels

MARGARET FENSOM

TIME

Time changes me
wastes me, enriches,
as I add poem to poem
and all the days and deeds of my life.

I carry time with me:
its wristwatch agent
reflects the sun on fences as I pass
and the unseen trail
of me through space-time
and crossing countless other trails:
same place, another time,
same time, another place,
weaves a pattern
into the universal cloth.

MARGARET FENSOM

LIFE

an illusion
I reinvent
every morning

no

life is

an illusion
I recreate
every moment

G.M. WALKER

LESSONS
For little Matty

Lessons bloom like flowers grey;
grainy, gritty, lessons may,
lead-like even, puncture perfect day
or, lead the seed that's grown astray.

PEACH HOWEY-LENIXXH

FISH EYES

fish eyes fall from sky
humans squash them underfoot
day and night and week and month
fish eyes fall on everyone
some new turn up for the book
only history will complain
why fish eyes fall as rain
and cadence comes upon the wind
to sweep this plague aside
and what remains when eyes subside
without a reason to explain and
no one left to question why
the fish eyes fell from sky

ALAN P. KELLY
Read at the Port Adelaide Festival, October 2009

TO THE FISH

To the fish
as it flips its fin
to the eye of the tree
up high
higher than it can ever be

ah that blossom
tipples the sun
in its finger dance
out of its world
but for the bird
who touches them both.

ROS SCHULZ
Mentored Poet 2009

SWEET RIFF

Come to me like the gully breeze
blessed in the steaming summer night,
let's keep the world out between our four arms –
and the band will play a sweet, sweet riff

and then maybe another till the end of time
it's all turning and twisting into dreams,
that frug and waltz and cartwheel,
but the band play a sweet, sweet riff

which will last us our whole life long,
over the oil-stain darkness
out there on the clawing streets –
the band will play a sweet, sweet riff

and the chorus make love to the solo-break,
the charts are heavily involved with the parts
all winds and strings and skins –
ah, and the band will play a sweet, sweet riff;

so the stories will all be good,
the band will play a sweet, sweet riff
dancing hands and leaping hearts:
the band will play a sweet, sweet riff!

AVALANCHE

EARTH'S HOUR

Fine spangled robes of blue and green adorn
her ancient mass, primeval lump of rock.
Upon her sleeping form, before the morn,
lace lights are set, like sequins on a frock.
Her cities shimmer, all on edge, awake
to business, bustle, nervous pulsing power,
but for one hour, in shadow we forsake
light. We talk and touch, we smell each flower.
We cry. We cannot let our sparkling pearl
return to rock, our precious children die.
How small this blue green planet all awhirl.
How vulnerable, how fragile. We must try.
This is the singing of a simple song.
A simple choice. Shall we reverse the wrong?

JACQUI MERCKENSCHLAGER
Read at Murray Bridge, September 2009

UNTITLED 32

Surviving through
to healing and thriving
the kitchen-talking cure,
the confrontation of panic attack,
for fear of confronting the really confrontable,
the risk of losing more friends,
never time to run primal in the park
coming home with a veteran's varnish
the planet pleads a wheelchair invalidation
as new technology permeates the sedentary psyche
however, much history it takes to boil an egg
a final analysis lifts the lid off
exposure and association
reeling off
like life-lines
passed through tubular hands
to the harnessed heroes heaving though surf
names and faces
people and places
case-notes and cases
escapes and chases
bootstraps and laces
veils lighting inevitable, inexorable
rising,
revealing stages,
at levels of action and statis,
lines of genomic force unraveling
defragging connective tissue electronically
blessing the breathing around the sneezing.

KAHLIL JUREIDINI

ADCE PRESENT / BCE PRE_SENT: TIME CONTINUUM

Eastrogen and Westrogen
'n' Sustagen and Milo
wrap it up in balls of light
and put it inner sigh low
quantum and strontium
and black holes / worm holes / Lithium and Bling!
    ... These are some clues
      to the whole fucking thing!?

Jesus, Mohammed and Buddha, Slim Pickens
chickens and dickens and fingertip lickin's
Strangelove and Grange love, *Enola Gay* sickens
nuclear toy-boys and girls playing war?
Hiroshima's legacy now just a bore?!
Can you balance wasted talents
speaking truth to power?
And ... will they listen,
swap killin' for kissin'
and conquer the hard rain shower!!!

All these so called 'black' holes
are they really 'collapsars'?
Steve Hawking's just jawking
with lightspeed and tramcars
optic nerve barcodes
plugged into the brain
vortex on matrix / matrix on vortex
flushed down Darwin's drain
    what's the answer, what's the secret,
    to the universe
I really must know now
unfurrow my brow now
this must not get any worse!

Riddle-me riddle-me, ole uncle Remus
Brer Bear, Brer Rabbit and Brer Fox the shamus
investigating the whole living world
into which, somehow, we all have been hurled

Politicians! and technicians! and
all you science (fans! dons! nuts!)
I'll solve the blindspot
and can we cure brainrot?
Now, all go and Find Your G.U.T.S!

KAHLIL JUREIDINI

For further information about
Friendly Street publications and activities please visit
our website: friendlystreetpoets.org.au
email: poetry@friendlystreetpoets.org.au
postal: PO Box 3697 Norwood SA 5067